Reading/Writing Companion

Mc
Graw
Hill

mheducation.com/prek-12

Send all inquiries to:
McGraw Hill
1325 Avenue of the Americas
New York, NY 10019

ISBN: 978-1-26-573879-2
MHID: 1-26-573879-3

Printed in the United States of America.

3 4 5 6 7 8 9 LWI 26 25 24 23 22   A

Welcome to
WONDERS!

We're here to help you set goals to build on the amazing things you already know. We'll also help you reflect on everything you'll learn.

Let's start by taking a look at the incredible things you'll do this year.

You'll build knowledge on exciting topics and find answers to interesting questions.

You'll read fascinating fiction, informational texts, and poetry and respond to what you read with your own thoughts and ideas.

And you'll research and write stories, poems, and essays of your own!

Here's a sneak peek at how you'll do it all.

"Let's go!"

You'll explore new ideas by reading groups of different texts about the same topic. These groups of texts are called *text sets*.

At the beginning of a text set, we'll help you set goals on the My Goals page. You'll see a bar with four boxes beneath each goal. Think about what you already know to fill in the bar. Here's an example.

I can read and understand realistic fiction.

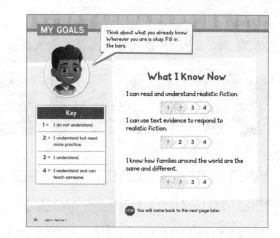

As you move through a text set, you'll explore an essential question and build your knowledge of a topic until you're ready to write about it yourself.

You'll also learn skills that will help you reach your text set goals. At the end of lessons, you'll see a new Check In bar with four boxes.

CHECK IN ▸ 1 ❯ 2 ❯ 3 ❯ 4 ❯

Reflect on how well you understood a lesson to fill in the bar.

Here are some questions you can ask yourself.

- Was I able to complete the task?

- Was it easy or was it hard?

- Do I think I need more practice?

You have plenty of tools and resources to learn more, such as anchor charts and center activities. You can also reread a lesson or ask a teacher or peer for help.

At the end of each text set, you'll show off the knowledge you built by completing a fun task. Then you'll return to the second My Goals page where we'll help you reflect on all that you learned.

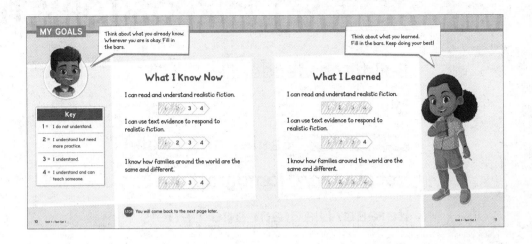

TEXT SET 1 **EXPOSITORY TEXT**

TEXT SET 2 **FABLE**

TEXT SET 3 **POETRY**

UNIT 2

EXTENDED WRITING

CONNECT AND REFLECT

 Digital Tools

Find this eBook and other resources at **my.mheducation.com.**

wavebreakmedia/Shutterstock

Build Knowledge

? Essential Question

How are offspring like
their parents?

Build Vocabulary

Write new words you learned about animal parents and their offspring. Draw lines and circles for the words you write.

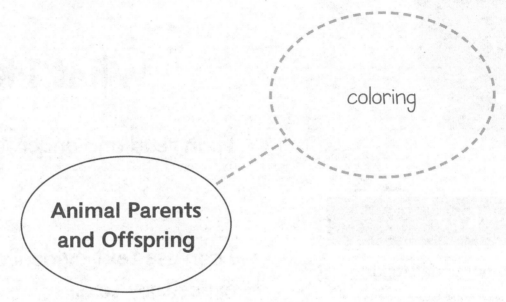

coloring

Animal Parents and Offspring

Go online to **my.mheducation.com** and read the "Amazing Animal Parents" Blast. Think about how animal parents care for their offspring. Then blast back your response.

Think about what you already know. Wherever you are is okay. Fill in the bars.

Key

1 = I do not understand.

2 = I understand but need more practice.

3 = I understand.

4 = I understand and can teach someone.

What I Know Now

I can read and understand expository text.

1 > 2 > 3 > 4

I can use text evidence to respond to expository text.

1 > 2 > 3 > 4

I know about how offspring are like their parents.

1 > 2 > 3 > 4

 STOP You will come back to the next page later.

Think about what you learned. Fill in the bars. Keep doing your best!

What I Learned

I can read and understand expository text.

| 1 | 2 | 3 | 4 |

I can use text evidence to respond to expository text.

| 1 | 2 | 3 | 4 |

I know about how offspring are like their parents.

| 1 | 2 | 3 | 4 |

My Goal I can read and understand expository text.

TAKE NOTES

As you read, write down interesting words and important information.

_____

_____

_____

_____

_____

_____

Eagles and Eaglets

Essential Question

?

How are offspring like their parents?

Read to learn how young bald eagles are like their parents.

Bald eagles are birds. The baby birds, or **offspring** are called eaglets. Let's read about how eaglets are like their parents.

It's Nesting Time

All birds lay eggs. Bald eagles build their nests in the tops of trees so the eggs will be safe. Their nests are built of sticks and grass. They add on to their nests each year. They can become huge! These **giant** nests can be as large as nine feet across. That's bigger than your bed!

The mother eagle lays from one to three eggs. She sits on her eggs until they hatch. Then both parents watch over the nest.

EXPOSITORY TEXT

FIND TEXT EVIDENCE

Read

Paragraph 1
Reread
Reread and **underline** the sentence that explains what an eaglet is.

Paragraphs 2-3
Central Idea and Details
Circle the sentence that tells how eagles keep their eggs safe. What happens after the eggs hatch?

_____

_____

_____

Reread
Author's Craft

How does the author help you to picture the size of an eagle's nest?

FIND TEXT EVIDENCE

Read

Paragraph 1

Central Idea and Details

Underline two ways eaglets need their parents.

Paragraph 2

Reread

Circle what eagles use to hunt, fly, and catch fish.

Homographs

In the last sentence, does *live* mean "to happen now" or "to stay alive"?

_____

_____

Reread

Author's Craft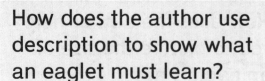

How does the author use description to show what an eaglet must learn?

Proud Parents

At first the eaglets are helpless. They cannot walk. They need their parents for food. They also cannot see well. Birds are not **mammals**. They do not have milk to feed their young. They hunt for food. Eaglets also need their parents for safety.

Eaglets Grow Up

Bald eagles use their sharp eyes to hunt. They use their strong wings to fly fast. They also use their claws and beak to catch fish. Young eaglets must learn all these things. Then they can live on their own.

The eagles must bring food to the eaglets.

Accent Alaska.com/Alamy Stock Photo

Unlike mammals, birds have feathers, not **fur**. An eaglet is born **covered** with soft gray down. It cannot fly until it grows dark feathers like its parents. The eaglet stays near the nest until its wings grow strong. That takes about five months.

Bald Eagle

powerful eyes

dark feathers on body and wings

hooked yellow beak

white tail feathers

long claws

Frank Leung/E+/Getty Images

FIND TEXT EVIDENCE

Read

Central Idea and Details
Underline the text that tells when eaglets can fly. How long does it take for their wings to grow strong?

_____

_____

_____

_____

Diagram and Labels
Circle the part of the diagram that shows what eagles use to fly.

FIND TEXT EVIDENCE 🔍

`Read`

Reread

Underline the sentence that tells you when an eaglet becomes an adult. **Circle** how long this takes.

`Reread`

Author's Craft

How does the author point out an important detail in the illustration?

An eaglet becomes an **adult** when it has learned to do all the things its parents do. This takes about five years. Bald eagles can stay **alive** for up to thirty years.

When the bald eagle soars, the feathers on its huge wings spread out like fingers.

Bald Eagles Soar

Once it learns to fly, the bald eagle can soar for hours. The bald eagle must take good care of its feathers. It uses its beak to **groom** itself. It must keep its feathers clean. Can you believe this powerful eagle began life as a helpless baby?

Ken Canning/E+/Getty Images

Retell

Look at your notes and think about the facts in "Eagles and Eaglets." Then retell the most important information.

FIND TEXT EVIDENCE

Read

Central Idea and Details
What can a bald eagle do once it learns to fly?

_____

_____

Homographs
Underline two sentences that help you understand the meaning of *groom*. What does an eagle use to groom its feathers?

_____

Reread

Author's Craft

Reread the last sentence. How does the author use a question and word choice to make you think about important information?

Vocabulary

**Talk with a partner about each word.
Then answer the questions.**

adult

My father is an adult.

Who are some adults that you know?

_____

_____

alive

I water the flowers to keep them alive.

What are some things that are alive?

_____

_____

covered

An eagle is covered with feathers.

What is a place in your town covered with grass?

_____

_____

fur

My kitten has fur that is soft and fluffy.

Name some other animals that have fur.

_____

_____

giant

An elephant is a giant animal.

What other animals are giant?

_____

_____

Build Your Word List Reread the
second paragraph on page 13.
Circle *huge*. Write synonyms for *huge*.
Use a thesaurus to help you.

groom

I use a brush to **groom** my dog.

How does a cat groom itself?

_____

_____

mammal

A **mammal** is an animal that has fur or hair and breathes air.

What mammals can you name?

_____

_____

offspring

The mother rabbit has two **offspring**.

What is the name for the offspring of a dog?

_____

_____

Homographs

Homographs are words that are spelled the same but have different meanings and sometimes different pronunciations.

🔍 **FIND TEXT EVIDENCE**

I know down _can mean "to go from high to low" or "fluffy feathers." Since eaglets are covered with down, the second meaning makes sense in this sentence._

An eaglet is born covered with soft gray (down.)

Your Turn Use clues on page 13 to figure out the meaning of _hatch_ in the text.

_____

_____

CHECK IN 1 > 2 > 3 > 4

Takayuki Maekawa/The Image Bank/Getty Images

Reread

As you read, you may come across new words or information you don't understand. You can reread to help you understand the text.

 FIND TEXT EVIDENCE

On page 14 of "Eagles and Eaglets," the text tells how birds are helpless. I will go back and reread to understand why they are helpless.

Page 14

At first the eaglets are helpless. They cannot walk. They need their parents for food. They also cannot see well. Birds are not **mammals**. They do not have milk to feed their young. They hunt for food. Eaglets also need their parents for safety.

I reread that eaglets cannot walk, so they need their parents to get them food. This explains why they are helpless.

 Your Turn Why are eagles not able to fly when they are born? Reread page 15 to find the answer.

CHECK IN 1 2 3 4

Diagram and Labels

The selection "Eagles and Eaglets" is an expository text. It gives facts about a topic and has text features.

🔍 FIND TEXT EVIDENCE

I know that "Eagles and Eaglets" is an expository text because it gives facts about eagles. It also has text features that help me learn about eagles. I see a diagram and labels.

Page 15

Unlike mammals, birds have feathers, not **fur**. An eaglet is born **covered** with soft gray down. It cannot fly until it grows dark feathers like its parents. The eaglet stays near the nest until its wings grow strong. That takes about five months.

Bald Eagle

powerful eyes

dark feathers on body and wings

hooked yellow beak

white tail feathers

long claws

Diagram

A diagram is a picture that shows information.

Labels

The labels explain parts of the diagram.

Your Turn What did you learn about eagles from looking at the diagram and reading the labels?

_____

_____

CHECK IN 1 2 3 4

Central Idea and Relevant Details

Steve Shuey/Alamy Stock Photo

The central idea is the most important point an author has about a topic. A relevant detail is important information that supports the central idea.

FIND TEXT EVIDENCE

On page 13, I read information about an eagle's giant nest. I understand that a relevant detail about eagles and eaglets is that the parents take care of their eggs and offspring in the nest.

Detail

Eagles build a giant nest where they take care of their young.

Quick Tip

Think about what the details have in common, or what they all tell about. This will help you to identify the author's central idea about the topic.

Your Turn Continue reading the text. Fill in the graphic organizer with relevant details and the central idea.

CHECK IN ⟩ 1 ⟩ 2 ⟩ 3 ⟩ 4 ⟩

Detail

Eagles build a giant nest where they take care of their young.

Detail

Detail

Central Idea

I can use text evidence to respond to expository text.

Respond to Reading

COLLABORATE

Talk about the prompt below. Use your notes and text evidence to support your ideas.

Why do eagles need to take care of their offspring?

_____

_____

_____

_____

_____

_____

_____

_____

Quick Tip

Use these sentence starters to help you organize your text evidence.

An eaglet cannot...

An eaglet learns to...

An eaglet grows...

Grammar Connections

Remember that nouns name people, places, and things. Try to use specific nouns that will help a reader understand your ideas.

CHECK IN   1   2   3   4

Life Cycle Diagram

COLLABORATE

Create a diagram that shows the life cycle of an insect. Follow the research process to create your diagram.

Step 1 **Set a Goal** Decide on an insect for the diagram.

The Life Cycle of a(n) _____

Step 2 **Identify Sources** Find sources of information about the insect. Your sources can be books from the library or websites on the Internet.

Write a source: _____

_____

Step 3 **Find and Record Information** When you do Internet research, remember to use keywords to tell the search engine what to look for. Write down facts and draw pictures for each stage of the life cycle.

Step 4 **Organize and Combine Information** Put details about the stages in order, or sequence. Think about adding a number to each stage.

Step 5 **Create and Present** Illustrate and add arrows to the final diagram. Take turns presenting the stages in the life cycle diagram to the class.

Quick Tip

Use websites that you can trust for your sources. School websites that end in ".edu" or government websites that end in ".gov" are good choices. Avoid doing research on websites that try to convince you of an opinion.

Hintau Aliaksei/Shutterstock

CHECK IN 1 > 2 > 3 > 4

Baby Bears

*Literature Anthology:
pages 110–127*

? **How does the author use photographs and captions to help you understand bear families?**

Talk About It Talk about the details in the photographs and caption on pages 118–119.

Cite Text Evidence Write what you learn about bear families from the text, photographs, and caption.

Text	Photographs	Caption

Make Inferences

Think about what bears must learn in order to live on their own. What inference can you make about why bear cubs need to learn to climb trees?

Write The author uses photographs and captions _____

CHECK IN 1 2 3 4

? **How does the author use headings to show how the text is organized?**

Talk About It Reread page 120. Talk about the question that the heading at the top of the page asks.

Cite Text Evidence Write the heading on page 120. Then write details from this part, or section, of the text.

Use the sentence starters to discuss the section of text.

Most bears eat…

Polar bears are…

Pandas are…

Combine Information

Reread page 121. Why does the author mention that bamboo grows in the panda's habitat?

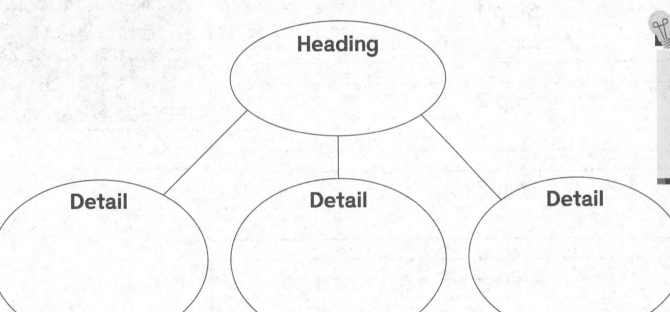

Heading

Detail

Detail

Detail

Write The author uses headings to show _____

_____

? **How does the diagram help you understand how baby bears become adult bears?**

COLLABORATE

Talk About It Reread page 124 of the **Literature Anthology**. Talk about how a cub becomes an adult.

Cite Text Evidence Write the steps in a bear's life cycle.

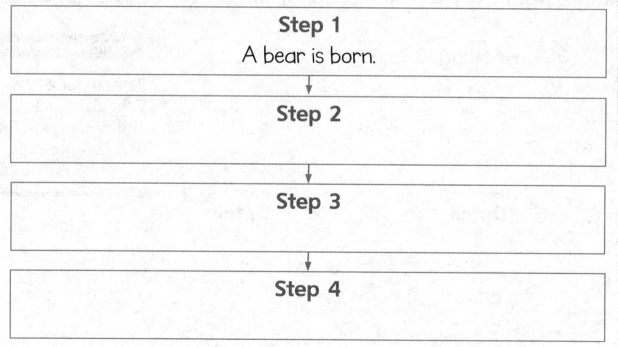

Step 1
A bear is born.

↓

Step 2

↓

Step 3

↓

Step 4

Write The diagram helps me understand how _____

_____

_____

CHECK IN 〉 1 〉 2 〉 3 〉 4 〉

Respond to Reading

My Goal I can use text evidence to respond to expository text.

Discuss the prompt below. Use your notes and text evidence to support your response.

Why do baby bears need to stay with their mothers?

_____

_____

_____

_____

_____

_____

_____

_____

Quick Tip

Use these sentence starters to organize your text evidence.

Baby bears nurse...

The mother teaches...

The cubs stay to...

Young bears grow...

CHECK IN ⟩ 1 ⟩ 2 ⟩ 3 ⟩ 4 ⟩

From Caterpillar to Butterfly

A butterfly is not a mammal. It does not have live babies or feed milk to its young. A butterfly is an insect. It lays eggs.

Lee Canfield/SuperStock

Literature Anthology: pages 128–129

Reread the title and text. What does the title tell you about the topic of the selection?

_____

_____

_____

_____

_____

Circle details that explain what a butterfly is.

COLLABORATE

Discuss the photo on the page. What does it show? How does the photo support the topic?

Butterfly Life Cycle

1. Egg
The adult butterfly lays an egg on a milkweed leaf.

2. Larva
After 3 or 4 days, a tiny caterpillar comes out of the egg. Caterpillars are a kind of larva. The caterpillar eats its shell for food.

3. Caterpillar
For about two weeks, the caterpillar eats leaves and grows bigger.

4. Chrysalis
The caterpillar forms a shell around itself. The shell is called a chrysalis.

5. Adult
Two weeks later, an adult butterfly comes out of the chrysalis. It will lay an egg on a leaf, and the cycle will continue.

Reread the page. What happens first in the life cycle of a butterfly? How do you know?

_____

_____

_____

_____

_____

Reread step 4. **Underline** the sentence that tells what a chrysalis is. **Circle** the chrysalis in the life cycle.

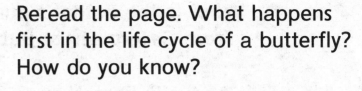

COLLABORATE

Discuss how the writer organizes the information in a diagram. Use text evidence to support your response.

(tl)Ingram Publishing/Alamy Stock Photo; (tc)Ed Reschke/Photolibrary/Getty Images; (tr,b)Don Johnston_lH/Alamy Stock Photo; (br)U.S. Fish & Wildlife Service

What is the author's purpose for writing "From Caterpillar to Butterfly"?

COLLABORATE

Talk About It Reread page 31. Why are the parts of the diagram numbered? What do the parts show?

Cite Text Evidence Write clues in the diagram of a butterfly life cycle that show the author's purpose.

Quick Tip

Headings in the diagram name each stage. The photographs show what the stages look like.

Clue	Clue

Author's Purpose

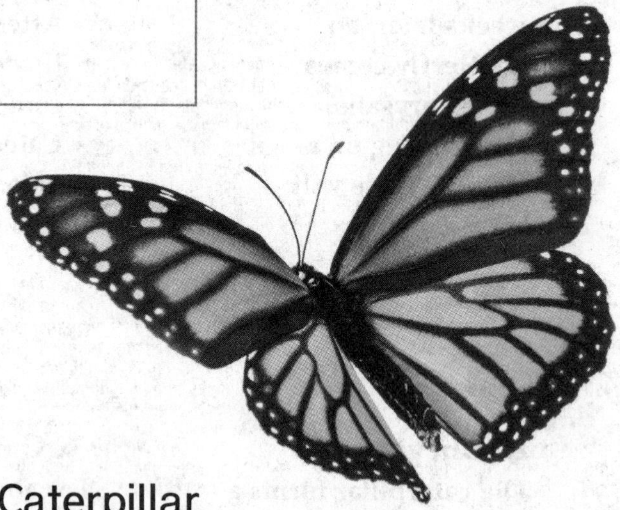

Write The author's purpose in writing "From Caterpillar to Butterfly" is ______________________________

____

____

CHECK IN 1 2 3 4

Diagrams

Authors can use diagrams to show how parts of something work together. Life cycle diagrams show and tell how living things grow and change.

 FIND TEXT EVIDENCE
Look back at the butterfly life cycle diagram again on page 31. Take notes on each step on the lines below.

1. _____

2. _____

3. _____

4. _____

5. Two weeks later, an adult butterfly comes out.

 Your Turn Why does the author show the life cycle of a butterfly in a circle?

_____

_____

You can use diagrams to explain important details and show how they are connected. Adding arrows and numbers to your diagram can help show how the parts work together or follow a sequence.

? **What does the photograph of the sculpture help you understand? How are these ideas similar to what you learned in "Eagles and Eaglets" and *Baby Bears*?**

COLLABORATE

Talk About It Talk about the sculpture and caption. What does the artist show about a mother lion and her cubs, or offspring?

Cite Text Evidence In the caption, **underline** a clue that tells how long the cubs need their mother.

Write The selections I read and the sculpture and caption help me understand how baby animals

_____

_____

_____

_____

_____

_____

Use these sentence starters as you talk about the sculpture and answer the question.

Baby animals need their parents for...

The offspring, or babies, must learn...

The artist shows lion cubs clinging to their mother. The cubs need her until they learn to hunt for themselves.

CHECK IN 1 2 3 4

My Goal I know about how offspring are like their parents.

Make a Picture Book

Think about how the young animals you read about grow. Think about ways they are not like their parents. How do they change and become adults? Show how three young animals grow up to be like their parents.

1 Look at your Build Knowledge notes in your reader's notebook.

2 Create a picture book that shows how three young animals change. Illustrate your book with drawings or photographs. Write captions that describe how each offspring becomes an adult.

3 Include some of the new words you learned. Use examples from at least three texts you read.

Think about what you learned in this text set. Fill in the bars on page 11.

Build Knowledge

What can animals in stories teach us?

Build Vocabulary

Write new words you learned from the lessons taught in stories with animals. Draw lines and circles for the words you write.

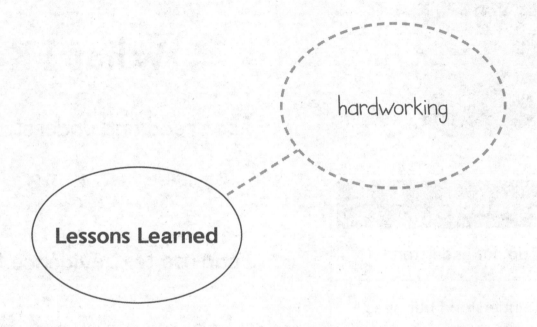

hardworking

Lessons Learned

Go online to **my.mheducation.com** and read the "Creatures as Teachers" Blast. Think about how animal characters are used in Aesop's fables. Then blast back your response.

Think about what you already know. Fill in the bars. There are no wrong answers here.

What I Know Now

Key
1 = I do not understand.
2 = I understand but need more practice.
3 = I understand.
4 = I understand and can teach someone.

I can read and understand a fable.

> 1 > 2 > 3 > 4 >

I can use text evidence to respond to a fable.

> 1 > 2 > 3 > 4 >

I know about what animals in stories can teach us.

> 1 > 2 > 3 > 4 >

STOP You will come back to the next page later.

Think about what you learned. Fill in the bars. What helped you the most?

What I Learned

I can read and understand a fable.

1 > 2 > 3 > 4

I can use text evidence to respond to a fable.

1 > 2 > 3 > 4

I know about what animals in stories can teach us.

1 > 2 > 3 > 4

My Goal I can read and understand a fable.

TAKE NOTES

As you read, write down interesting words and important events.

_____

_____

_____

_____

_____

_____

_____

The Boy Who Cried Wolf

Essential Question

?

What can animals in stories teach us?

Read to find out what a shepherd boy learns.

Long ago a shepherd boy sat on a hilltop watching the village sheep. He was not **fond** of his job. He didn't like it one bit. He would have liked something wonderful to happen, but nothing **remarkable** ever did.

The shepherd boy watched the clouds move softly by to stay busy. He saw horses, dogs, and dragons in the sky. He made up **stories** with these things as characters.

Peter Francis

FIND TEXT EVIDENCE

Read

Paragraph 1

Plot: Sequence of Events

Circle the sentence that tells what problem the shepherd boy has first.

Paragraph 2

Character

Underline what the shepherd boy watches instead of the village sheep. Why does the boy make up stories?

The shepherd boy is bored.

Reread

Author's Craft

Why does the author include details about what the shepherd boy does and how he feels at his job?

FIND TEXT EVIDENCE

Read

Paragraph 2
Antonyms

Find and **circle** words with opposite meanings of *weeping* and *up*.

Paragraph 2
Make, Confirm, Revise Predictions

What do you think the boy will do next?

The boy will try to trick the vill

Then one day he had a better idea! He took a deep breath and cried out, "Wolf! Wolf! The wolf is chasing the sheep!"

The villagers ran up the hill to help the boy. When they got there, they saw no harmful wolf. The boy laughed. "Shepherd boy! Don't cry 'wolf!' unless there really is a wolf!" said the villagers. They went back down the hill.

That afternoon the boy again cried out, "Wolf! Wolf! The wolf is chasing the sheep!"

The villagers ran to help the boy again. They saw no wolf. The villagers were angry. "Don't cry 'wolf!' when there is NO WOLF!" they said. The shepherd boy just smiled. The villagers went quickly down the hill again.

Peter Francis

FIND TEXT EVIDENCE 🔍

Read

Paragraphs 1–2
Plot: Sequence of Events
Underline what the boy does that afternoon. **Circle** what happens when the villagers see no wolf.

Paragraphs 1–2
Make, Confirm, Revise Predictions
What do you think will happen next?

_____

_____

_____

Reread

Author's Craft

How do the text and illustrations show the villagers' feelings?

FIND TEXT EVIDENCE 🔍

Read

Paragraph 1

Make, Confirm, Revise Predictions

Was your prediction from page 43 correct? Why or why not?

_____

_____

Paragraph 2

Character

Circle the description of the boy. **Underline** the question that shows he does not understand how he made the villagers feel.

Reread

Author's Craft

How does the author use exclamation points to show how the boy feels?

That afternoon the boy saw a REAL wolf. He did not want the wolf to grab any of the sheep! The boy thought the wolf would **snatch** one of them for a **delicious**, tasty meal. A sheep would be a big **feast** for a wolf. He quickly jumped to his feet and cried, "WOLF! WOLF!" The villagers thought he was tricking them again, so they did not come.

That night the shepherd boy did not return with their sheep. The villagers found the boy weeping real tears. "There really was a wolf here!" he said. "The flock ran away! When I cried out, 'Wolf! Wolf!' no one came. Why didn't you come?"

A kind man talked to the boy as they walked slowly back to the village. "In the morning, we'll help you look for the sheep," he said. "You have just learned one of life's important **lessons**. This is something you need to know. Nobody **believes** a person who tells lies. It is always better to tell the truth!"

Peter Francis

Retell

Use your notes and think about what the characters say and do. Retell important events in the order they happen in the fable.

FIND TEXT EVIDENCE

Read

Plot: Sequence of Events
Circle who helps the boy at the end of the story. How does he help?

_____

_____

Combine Information
Use details you already know to explain how the boy learns his lesson.

_____

_____

Reread

Author's Craft

What message, or lesson, does the author want to share in this fable?

Vocabulary

Talk with a partner about each word. Then answer the questions.

believe

We **believe** it is going to rain today.

What is something you believe will happen today?

_____

_____

delicious

We ate the **delicious** pizza.

Describe something that tastes delicious.

_____

_____

> ✏️ **Build Your Word List** Reread the last paragraph on page 42. Circle _help_. Use a word web to write more forms of the word. Use a dictionary to help you.

feast

Our family has a **feast** on holidays.

When do you have a feast?

_____

_____

fond

Rob is very **fond** of his puppy.

What is something that you are fond of?

_____

_____

lessons

You learn important **lessons** from your family.

What lessons do you learn at school?

_____

_____

remarkable

I saw a **remarkable** rainbow after the rain.

Describe something that is remarkable.

_____

_____

snatch

My dog can **snatch** a ball out of the air.

Show how you would snatch something from your desk.

_____

_____

stories

Dad reads **stories** before bedtime.

What are some stories you like?

_____

_____

Antonyms

Antonyms are words that are opposite in meaning.

🔍 FIND TEXT EVIDENCE

As I read, I see the words lies *and* truth. *I can tell they have opposite meanings from details in the story. This helps me to understand what each antonym means.*

Nobody believes a person who tells lies. It is always better to tell the truth!

Your Turn Find the antonym for this word.

morning, page 45 _____

Use a pair of antonyms to write your own sentence in your reader's notebook.

CHECK IN ⟩ 1 ⟩ 2 ⟩ 3 ⟩ 4 ⟩

Make, Confirm, Revise Predictions

Quick Tip

The author tells how the boy does the same thing over and over again. Use this repeating structure to help you predict what will happen next. Confirm or correct any predictions you make.

Use what you read in the story to help you predict, or guess, what might happen next. As you read, check to see if your predictions are correct. If they are not correct, revise, or change, your predictions.

◯ FIND TEXT EVIDENCE

On page 42 of "The Boy Who Cried Wolf," I made a prediction about the boy's actions and what he will do next.

Page 43

That afternoon the boy again cried out, "Wolf! Wolf! The wolf is chasing the sheep!"

The villagers ran to help the boy again. They saw no wolf. The villagers were angry.

On page 43, I confirmed my prediction by reading about how the villagers react.

Your Turn When the boy saw the wolf, what did you predict would happen? Reread the text on page 44 and find the text that confirmed your prediction.

CHECK IN 1 2 3 4

Character

"The Boy Who Cried Wolf" is a made-up story called a fable. Fables teach a lesson. Character traits can be important details in teaching the fable's lesson.

FIND TEXT EVIDENCE

I can tell that "The Boy Who Cried Wolf" is a fable with a lesson at the end. The traits of a character lead to the lesson that the character learns.

Page 41

Long ago a shepherd boy sat on a hilltop watching the village sheep. He was not **fond** of his job. He didn't like it one bit. He would have liked something wonderful to happen, but nothing **remarkable** ever did.

The shepherd boy watched the clouds move softly by to stay busy. He saw horses, dogs, and dragons in the sky. He made up **stories** with these things as characters.

Quick Tip

Character traits are words that describe what a character is like. At the end of the story, we read about a "kind man." The word *kind* is a character trait. It tells what the man is like.

Character

The shepherd boy watches clouds instead of the sheep. He is not very responsible, or serious, at his job.

Your Turn Describe two traits of the boy from the middle of the fable. What leads to the lesson he learns at the end?

COLLABORATE

_____

_____

_____

CHECK IN 1 > 2 > 3 > 4

Plot: Sequence of Events

The sequence of events is the order that important events happen in a story. We can use the words *first, next, then,* and *last* to tell the order of what happens.

🔍 **FIND TEXT EVIDENCE**

As I read page 41 of "The Boy Who Cried Wolf," I see details in the illustrations and text that tell me about the first event in the story. The boy is bored at his job and watches the clouds in the sky.

Quick Tip

The author uses time words such as *that afternoon* or *that night* to describe a change in setting. Time words often begin a new event in the story.

> **First**
>
> The shepherd boy watches clouds because he is bored.

Your Turn Continue rereading "The Boy Who Cried Wolf." Fill in the graphic organizer to tell the sequence of events in the story.

CHECK IN ⟩ 1 ⟩ 2 ⟩ 3 ⟩ 4 ⟩

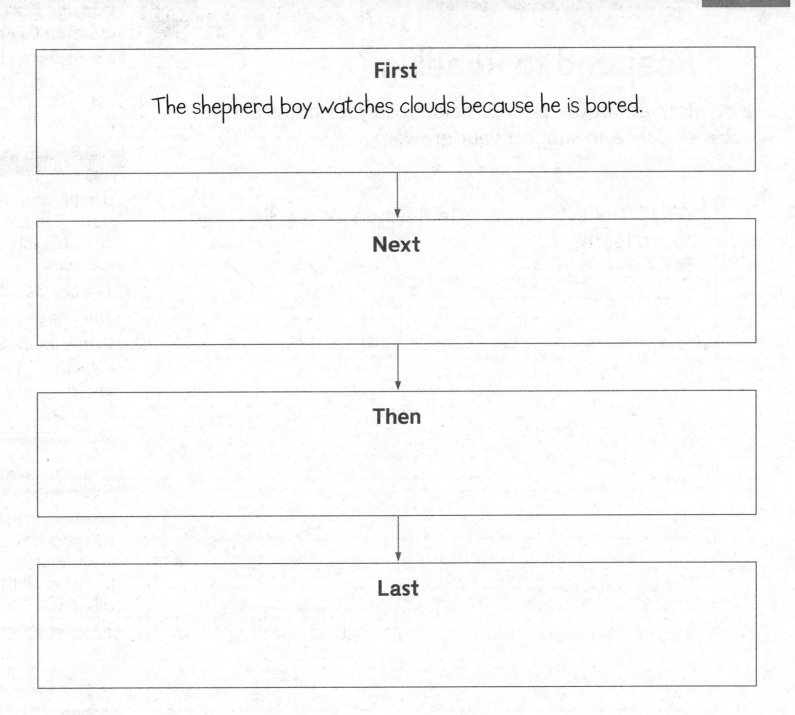

First

The shepherd boy watches clouds because he is bored.

↓

Next

↓

Then

↓

Last

Respond to Reading

Talk about the prompt below. Use your notes and text evidence to support your answer.

Why is honesty an important lesson for the shepherd boy to learn?

_____

_____

_____

_____

_____

_____

_____

_____

Quick Tip

Use these sentence starters to help you organize your text evidence.

The boy decides to…

The villagers are…

When a real wolf comes,…

The shepherd boy now feels…

Grammar Connections

Remember that *villagers* is plural, so use the pronoun *they* to talk about the villagers.

CHECK IN 1 2 3 4

Food Chain Diagram

With a partner, create a diagram that shows the food chain of a wolf. Follow the research process to create your diagram.

Step 1 **Set a Goal** Discuss what you know now about a wolf's food chain. Talk about what you want to learn more about. Write a research goal below.

_____

_____

_____

Step 2 **Identify Sources** Cite your sources, or tell where you find information. For a book, write the author, title, and year it was written.

Step 3 **Find and Record Information** Take notes on each link, or part, in the food chain.

Step 4 **Organize and Combine Information** Plan on how to clearly show the plants and animals in a diagram.

Step 5 **Create and Present** Illustrate and label your diagram. Share your work with the class.

Michelle Lalancette/Shutterstock

These wolves are looking for prey, such as a deer or moose, to eat.

CHECK IN ⟩ 1 ⟩ 2 ⟩ 3 ⟩ 4 ⟩

Wolf! Wolf!

? **How does the author help you understand how the wolf feels about the weeds in his garden?**

Literature Anthology: pages 130–153

Talk About It Reread page 131. What do the words and the illustration tell you about how the wolf feels?

Cite Text Evidence Write clues about how the wolf is feeling. Find text evidence to support your answer.

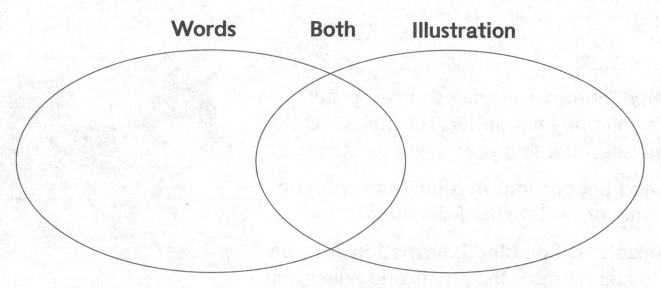

Words   Both   Illustration

Write The author helps me understand that the wolf _____

_____

_____

CHECK IN   1   2   3   4

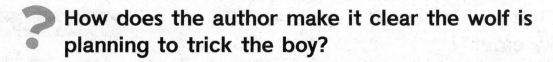
? How does the author make it clear the wolf is planning to trick the boy?

Talk About It Reread pages 143–145. Talk about what the wolf looks like and what he says when he meets the boy.

Cite Text Evidence Complete the chart. Write the clues that show you what the wolf is planning.

Illustration Clues	Text Clues

Write The author makes it clear that the wolf _____

_____

_____

_____

CHECK IN 1 2 3 4

? **Why does the author repeat the phrase "I'm a picky eater"?**

Talk About It Reread pages 145 and 149. Talk about what it means to be a picky eater.

Cite Text Evidence Write why both the wolf and the goat are picky eaters.

Wolf   **Both**   **Goat**

picky
eater

Write The author repeats the phrase "I'm a picky eater"

because _____

_____

_____

Quick Tip

Paying attention to how characters feel about each other helps you understand their actions. Once you know the wolf feels a connection with the goat, you understand why he doesn't eat him.

Evaluate Information

Reading and rereading the text carefully helps you gather evidence to support your ideas. What ideas do you have about how the characters act?

CHECK IN ⟩ 1 ⟩ 2 ⟩ 3 ⟩ 4 ⟩

Respond to Reading

COLLABORATE

Discuss the prompt below. Use your notes and text evidence to support your response.

Why does the wolf change from the beginning of the story to the end?

_____

_____

_____

_____

_____

_____

_____

_____

_____

_____

Quick Tip

Use these sentence starters to organize your text evidence.

At the beginning of the story, the wolf...

At the end of the story, the wolf...

Cinderella and Friends

Yeh-Shen's only friend is a beautiful fish. Every day, the fish comes out of the water to meet her. Yeh-Shen feeds the fish. When the fish dies, Yeh-Shen learns the fish bones are magical. Yeh-Shen makes a wish. She wants to go to the spring festival. The bones give her a beautiful dress and golden slippers to wear. At the festival, Yeh-Shen loses one of the slippers. The king finds the lost slipper. He says that he wants to marry the owner of the slipper. Many people try on the golden slipper. It only fits Yeh-Shen. She and the king become married, and they live happily ever after.

Alex Steele-Morgan

Literature Anthology:
pages 154-157

Reread the story. **Circle** the clue that explains why Yeh-Shen might be sitting by the river. How does the author use the illustration to help tell the story?

_____

_____

Draw a box around how Yeh-Shen is a good friend to the fish.

How does the fish help Yeh-Shen? **Underline** the clue.

COLLABORATE

Talk with a partner about why it is important to help a friend who has a problem.

Rhodopis is a poor servant girl. Her only friends are the birds, hippos, and

monkeys along the river. Rhodopis likes to sing and dance for them. The birds eat from her hand. A monkey sometimes sits on her shoulder. They love her. One evening, a bird snatches her slipper away. The bird flies over the king's castle and drops the slipper onto his throne. The king searches to find the owner of the slipper. When he finds Rhodopis, they fall in love and she becomes the queen.

Reread the story. **Underline** a clue about how Rhodopis is a good friend to the animals. What does this tell you about Rhodopis?

_____

_____

_____

Circle what happens to Rhodopis at the end of the story. Explain how an animal friend helps her to meet the king.

_____

_____

_____

COLLABORATE

Talk with a partner about how Yeh-Shen and Rhodopis are similar. How are they different?

Alex Steele-Morgan

? **Why does the author tell you about these two stories from "Cinderella and Friends"?**

Talk About It Reread pages 58–59. Talk about what the two stories have in common.

Cite Text Evidence Write details from each story that help you understand how animals can be good friends.

Yeh-Shen	Rhodopis

Write The author tells these two stories to show

_____

_____

CHECK IN 1 2 3 4

Author's Purpose

Authors organize information to help readers learn about a topic. Some authors compare and contrast things, or show how they are alike and different.

FIND TEXT EVIDENCE
Look at pages 154–157 in the **Literature Anthology**. Describe how the author organizes the information to

help readers understand the topic. _____

_____

_____

_____

Your Turn Why did the author organize "Cinderella and Friends" to include stories from different parts of the world? Write your answer on the lines below.

_____

_____

_____

As you read an expository text, think about how the author organizes the information. Think about how the organization helps you understand the author's purpose, or reason, for writing the text.

CHECK IN   1   2   3   4

MAKE CONNECTIONS

? **What lessons can animals in the stories you read or stories that are acted out teach you?**

COLLABORATE

Talk About It Talk about what animal faces you see in the photograph. Why is it helpful to see what animal characters look like when a story is acted out?

Cite Text Evidence In the caption, **underline** the purpose of the masks. **Circle** one of the masks. Tell your partner how the mask can be used to tell stories.

Write From the animal masks and the animal characters in the selections I read, I learn

_____

_____

_____

_____

_____

Quick Tip

Describe what you learned by using these sentence starters.

The masks show...

The animal characters taught me...

Storytellers in Panama use animal masks like these to help tell stories.

CHECK IN 1 > 2 > 3 > 4

My Goal I know about what animals in stories can teach us.

Create a Poster

Think about the animals in the fables you read. Think about their character traits, or words that describe what they are like. What did you learn from these characters in the fables?

1. Look at your Build Knowledge notes in your reader's notebook.

2. Illustrate a poster with three animals from fables. Write each character's name and words that describe the character. Then write what you learned from this animal character in the fable.

3. Include some of the new words you learned. Use examples and evidence from three of the fables you read.

Think about what you learned in this text set. Fill in the bars on page 39.

Build Knowledge

Jeffrey L. Rotman/Corbis Documentary/Getty Images

Build Vocabulary

Write new words you learned about what people love about animals. Draw lines and circles for the words you write.

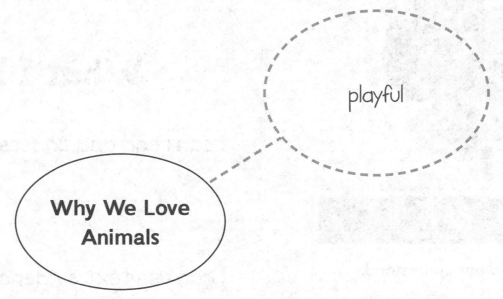

playful

Why We Love Animals

Go online to **my.mheducation.com** and read the "Dogs on the Job" Blast. Think about how dogs can do jobs to help people. Then blast back your response.

Think about what you already know. Fill in the bars. You'll keep learning more.

Key

1 = I do not understand.

2 = I understand but need more practice.

3 = I understand.

4 = I understand and can teach someone.

What I Know Now

I can read and understand poetry.

1 > 2 > 3 > 4

I can use text evidence to respond to poetry.

1 > 2 > 3 > 4

I know what we love about animals.

1 > 2 > 3 > 4

STOP You will come back to the next page later.

Think about what you learned. Fill in the bars. Keep up the good work!

What I Learned

I can read and understand poetry.

I can use text evidence to respond to poetry.

I know what we love about animals.

1 > 2 > 3 > 4

My Goal I can read and understand poetry.

TAKE NOTES

As you read, write down interesting words and details.

Cats and Kittens

Essential Question

? **What do we love about animals?**

Read how poets describe animals they love.

Cats and kittens express their views
With hisses, purrs, and little mews.

Instead of taking baths like me,
They use their tongues quite handily.

I wonder what my mom would say
If I tried cleaning up that way.

They stay as still as still can be,
Until a mouse they chance to see.

And then in one great flash of fur
They pounce on a toy with a PURRRR.

— by Constance Keremes

FIND TEXT EVIDENCE

Read

Lines 3–6
Theme

Underline the detail that tells how cats get clean. What does the narrator think about this?

(handwritten) IW
(handwritten) What

Lines 5–8
Rhyme Scheme

Circle the words that rhyme in lines 5–6. Then **draw a box** around words that rhyme in lines 7–8.

Reread

Author's Craft

How does the poet help the reader understand what kittens sound like?

Lines 1–2
Theme
Draw a box around how a camel's hump is used.

Line 5–6
Suffixes
Circle the word ending in the word that means "jump up and down." **Underline** what the word shows about the camels.

Alliteration
What three words in line 6 begin with the *s* sound?

Reread
Author's Craft

How does the poet show her feelings about camels?

Desert Camels

Camels have a hump on their backs
To carry people and their sacks.

They're very strong, don't mind the Sun,
Won't stop for drinks until they're done.

They give people a bouncy ride.
They sway and move from side to side.

I'd like a camel for a pet,
But haven't asked my mother yet!

— by Martine Wren

A Bat Is Not a Bird

A bat has neither feathers nor beak.
He does not chirp, just gives a shriek.

He flies by hearing sounds like pings,
Flapping, flapping his leathery wings.

At night when I'm asleep in my bed,
He gets to fly around instead!

— by Trevor Reynolds

Make Connections

Describe how you would behave with your favorite animal. How would the animal respond to you?

FIND TEXT EVIDENCE 🔍

Read

Lines 1–2
Theme
How does a bat look different from a bird?

_____

_____

_____

Lines 3-6
Rhyme Scheme
Underline the words that rhyme in lines 3 and 4.
Circle the words that rhyme in lines 5 and 6.

Reread

Author's Craft

How does the poet make a connection between the title of the poem and lines 1–2?

Vocabulary

Talk with a partner about each word. Then answer the questions.

behave

The boy is teaching his dog to **behave**.

How do you behave when you are in the library?

_____

_____

express

The dog wags its tail to **express** how it feels.

How do you express your feelings?

_____

_____

> **Build Your Word List** Pick a word from one of the poems and make a word web of different forms of the word.

feathers

A peacock is covered in colorful **feathers**.

Where else have you seen feathers?

_____

_____

flapping

The robin was **flapping** its wings quickly.

What bird have you seen flapping its wings?

_____

_____

Poetry Words

alliteration

Alliteration is the repeating of the beginning sound in words.

Write three words with the same beginning sound.

_____

_____

poem

A **poem** is a form of writing that expresses imagination or feelings.

Would you rather read a poem or a story? Why?

_____

_____

rhyme

When two words **rhyme**, they have the same ending sound.

What is a word that rhymes with *cat?*

_____

_____

rhythm

Rhythm is the repeating accents, or beats, in a poem.

Why would a poet want a poem to have rhythm?

_____

Suffixes

A suffix is a word part or syllable added to the end of a word. You can separate the base word from a suffix, such as light•ly, to figure out what the word means.

🔍 **FIND TEXT EVIDENCE**

I'm not sure what the word handily *means. The dictionary says that* handy *means "skillful at using something." The suffix —ly means "like" or "in a certain way." I think the word* handily *means "using something in a skillful way."*

They use their tongues quite handily.

Your Turn Use the suffix to figure out a word's meaning in "A Bat Is Not a Bird."

leathery, page 71 _____

_____

CHECK IN ⟩ 1 ⟩ 2 ⟩ 3 ⟩ 4 ⟩

Martin Poole/Digital Vision/Getty Images

Figurative Language: Alliteration

Alliteration can make a poem sound like music, or give it feeling. Alliteration can also make something described in a poem stand out to readers.

Quick Tip

A line of poetry has alliteration when two or more words begin with the same sound.

FIND TEXT EVIDENCE

Reread the lines from "Cats and Kittens." Think about how the poet uses alliteration when she describes cats.

Page 69

They stay as still as still can be,
Until a mouse they chance to see.

And then in one great flash of fur
They pounce on a toy with a PURRRR.

The poet uses alliteration to describe how cats can "stay as still as still can be." The words sound like music together and help me picture a cat standing very still.

Your Turn Find alliteration with the beginning *f* sound in "Cats and Kittens." What do the words describe, or help you to visualize?

_____

_____

_____

CHECK IN ▷ 1 ⟩ 2 ⟩ 3 ⟩ 4 ⟩

Rhyme Scheme

A rhyming poem tells a poet's thoughts or feelings. It has rhyming words that create a pattern, or rhyme scheme.

FIND TEXT EVIDENCE

I know "Cats and Kittens" is a rhyming poem. It tells the poet's thoughts about cats and has a pattern of rhymes.

Page 69

Cats and kittens express their views (A)
With hisses, purrs, and little mews. (A)

Instead of taking baths like me, (B)
They use their tongues quite handily. (B)

I wonder what my mom would say (C)
If I tried cleaning up that way. (C)

They stay as still as still can be, (D)
Until a mouse they chance to see. (D)

And then in one great flash of fur (E)
They pounce on a toy with a PURRRR. (E)

– by Constance Keremes

The last words of lines rhyme in a pattern, or a **rhyme scheme.** Capital letters show the rhyming lines. The letter *A* shows lines 1 and 2 rhyme.

Your Turn What is the rhyme scheme in "Desert Camels"? Mark capital letters after lines that rhyme on page 70. Then write the letters in a row to show the rhyme scheme.

_____

_____

_____

CHECK IN 1 > 2 > 3 > 4

Theme

The theme is the message, or big idea, that the poet wants to tell readers. Identifying the most important details in a poem can help you figure out the theme.

🔍 **FIND TEXT EVIDENCE**

As I read "Desert Camels," I learn how camels are strong. They can carry people and their sacks. I think this is a clue to the poem's theme.

Quick Tip

To decide if a detail is important, ask yourself if it helps you understand more about the topic of the poem.

Clue
Camels can carry heavy loads.

↓

Your Turn Reread "Desert Camels." Find two more clues and list them in the graphic organizer. Then write the poem's theme, or big idea, in the last box.

COLLABORATE

CHECK IN ⟩ 1 ⟩ 2 ⟩ 3 ⟩ 4 ⟩

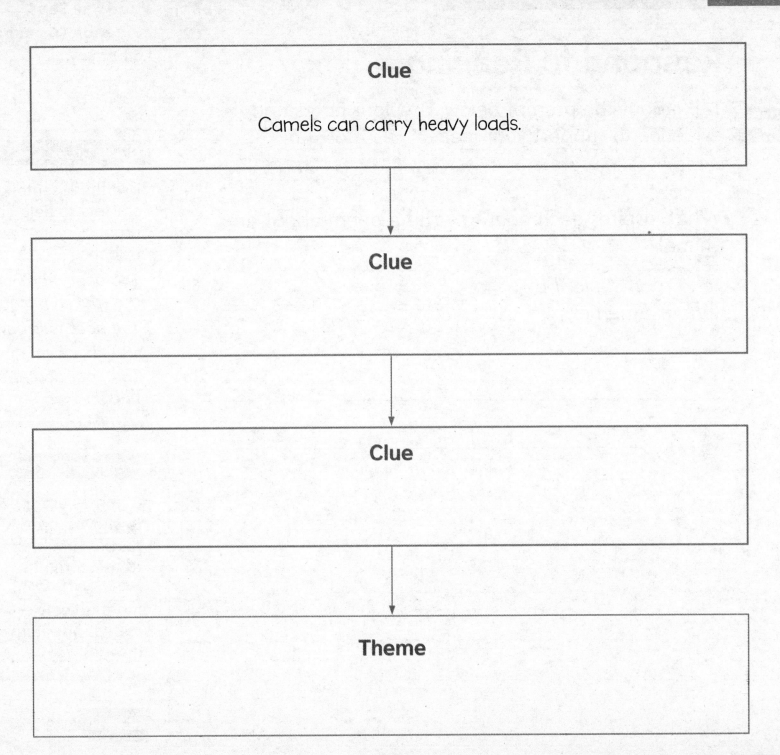

Clue

Camels can carry heavy loads.

Clue

Clue

Theme

My Goal
I can use text evidence to respond to poetry.

Respond to Reading

COLLABORATE

Talk about the prompt below. Use your notes and text evidence to support your ideas.

What inspires each poet to write a poem about an animal?

_____

_____

_____

_____

_____

_____

_____

CHECK IN 〉1 〉2 〉3 〉4 〉

Animal Information Cards

COLLABORATE
Create animal information cards about animals you read about. With a partner, follow the research process.

Step 1 **Set a Goal** For your topic, choose two animals that you find interesting and want to research.

Step 2 **Identify Sources** Think of questions about the basic needs of each animal. You may use books, magazines, and the Internet to find the answers. Write two of your questions below:

_____

_____

_____

Step 3 **Find and Record Information** Take notes in your own words. Write down, or cite, your sources.

Step 4 **Organize and Combine Information** Sort facts about the same ideas, such as where the animal lives, its diet, and how it stays safe.

Step 5 **Create and Present** Illustrate and label your cards. Then write information to present to the class on the back of each card.

What do most bats eat?

Where do bats sleep?

How do bats _____?

These are some questions a student wrote before starting research. Think about how the questions relate to the topic. What is another question the student could ask?

_____

_____

CHECK IN ⟩ 1 ⟩ 2 ⟩ 3 ⟩ 4

Literature Anthology:
pages 158–161

Beetles, The Little Turtle

How do the poets arrange the lines to show different patterns in the poems?

Talk About It Reread pages 159–160. Look at how the lines are placed. What patterns do you see?

Cite Text Evidence Write what you learned about how the poems look alike and different. Use the Venn diagram below.

Beetles	Both	The Little Turtle

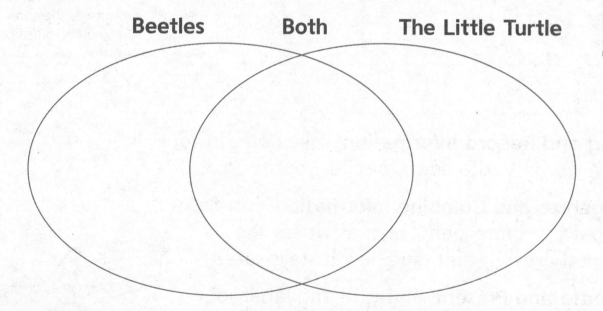

Write The lines are arranged to show _____

_____

CHECK IN 1 2 3 4

? **How does the poet use words to create rhythm in "The Little Turtle"?**

Talk About It Read the poem "The Little Turtle" aloud with a partner. Talk about how the poem sounds.

COLLABORATE

Cite Text Evidence Write the words that repeat and the words that rhyme in each stanza, or group of lines.

> **Quick Tip**
>
> Rhythm makes the lines in a poem fun to say. You say some words and parts of words more strongly than others. You can feel the rhythm as you read the lines.

Words that Repeat	Words that Rhyme
Stanza 1: _____ _____	Stanza 1: _____ _____
Stanza 2: _____ _____	Stanza 2: _____ _____
Stanza 3: _____ _____	Stanza 3: _____ _____

Write The poet creates rhythm by _____

_____

CHECK IN 1 2 3 4

Respond to Reading

Talk about the prompt below. Use your notes and text evidence to support your response.

COLLABORATE

How did the poems "Beetles" and "The Little Turtle" make you think or feel about the animals?

_____

_____

_____

_____

_____

_____

_____

Quick Tip

Use these sentence starters to organize your text evidence.

The poems made me think about...

In "Beetles," I could picture...

In "The Little Turtle," the turtle...

I can see the turtle...

CHECK IN > 1 > 2 > 3 > 4

Gray Goose

? How does the poet use rhythm to help you understand how the gray goose moves and feels?

COLLABORATE

Talk About It Talk about the fast rhythm of this poem. How does it fit with how the mama goose is feeling?

Literature Anthology: pages 162–163

Cite Text Evidence Write the words and phrases that describe how the mama goose moves in this poem.

Quick Tip

The illustrations can help you figure out and learn words you don't know.

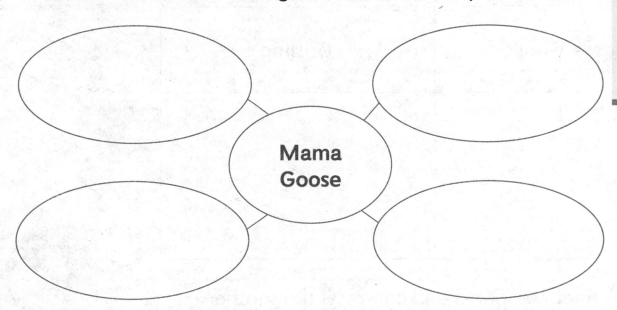

Mama Goose

Write The poet uses rhythm to help show

_____

_____

CHECK IN 1 2 3 4

? **How does the poet compare and contrast the mother goose and her gosling?**

Talk About It Reread page 162 and talk about what the mama goose does. What does the gosling do?

Cite Text Evidence Write the words describing the mama goose and the words describing the gosling in the chart below.

Mama Goose	Gosling

Write The poet compares and contrasts the mother goose and her gosling by showing _____

_____

CHECK IN 1 2 3 4

Lines and Line Breaks

The way a poem's lines are arranged, or placed, can add feeling and meaning to the words. Poets may break lines to create rhythm. A line break may also be used to give an important detail its own line.

FIND TEXT EVIDENCE

Take another look at the poem "Gray Goose" on page 162. What do you notice about the lines?

_____

_____

_____

Your Turn Read "Gray Goose" aloud to your partner. Listen to your partner read the poem. Why do you think the poet arranged the lines this way?

_____

_____

_____

Quick Tip

A "line break" is where a line ends for a new line to begin. As you read a poem, make a very short pause at the end of each line.

Readers to Writers

When you write your rhyming poem, the way you arrange the lines will affect how it looks and how it sounds.

CHECK IN 1 2 3 4

? **How do the authors of the poems you read help you understand how they feel about the animals?**

Talk About It Talk about what the speaker of "The Cow" loves about the animal.

Cite Text Evidence Circle sensory words in "The Cow." Sensory words appeal to the five senses, such as the sense of sight or sense of touch.

Write The poets of "Beetles," "Gray Goose," and "The Cow" use sensory

words to _____

_____

_____

_____

_____

_____

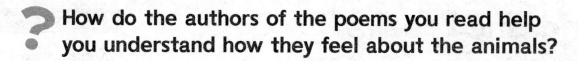

The Cow

The friendly cow all red and white,
    I love with all my heart:
She gives me cream with all her might,
    To eat with apple-tart.

She wanders lowing here and there,
    And yet she cannot stray,
All in the pleasant open air,
    The pleasant light of day;

And blown by all the winds that pass
    And wet with all the showers,
She walks among the meadow grass
    And eats the meadow flowers.

—by Robert Louis Stevenson

CHECK IN   1   2   3   4

I know what we love about animals.

Create a Puppet Show

Think about the animal poems you read. Think about how the poets describe the animals. What do the poets want their readers to think about?

1 Look at your Build Knowledge notes in your reader's notebook.

2 Create a puppet show with animals you read about in the poems. Write a conversation between three of the animals. Each animal describes details they like about another animal in a poem.

3 Include some of the new words you learned. Remember to use examples and evidence from three of the poems you read.

Think about what you learned in this text set. Fill in the bars on page 67.

Think about what you already know. Fill in the bars. Meeting your goals may take time.

Key
1 = I do not understand.
2 = I understand but need more practice.
3 = I understand.
4 = I understand and can teach someone.

What I Know Now

I can write a research report.

1 > 2 > 3 > 4

I can write a rhyming poem.

1 > 2 > 3 > 4

STOP You will come back to the next page later.

Think about what you learned. Fill in the bars. What do you want to work on more?

What I Learned

I can write a research report.

1 2 3 4

I can write a rhyming poem.

1 2 3 4

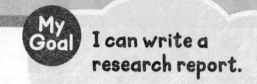

Expert Model

Features of a Research Report

A research report is a type of expository text. It gives ideas and information about a topic.

- It introduces the topic in the beginning.

- It has facts that tell about the topic.

- It can have a text structure that tells about things in order.

Literature Anthology: pages 110–127

Analyze an Expert Model Studying *Baby Bears* will help you learn to write a research report. Reread pages 112–113. Answer the questions below.

How does the author grab your attention?

_____

_____

How does the author introduce the topic of baby bears?

_____

_____

Word Wise

The author uses one sentence for each fact. This helps to make the information clear to the reader.

Plan: Brainstorm

Generate Ideas You will write a research report that tells how a baby animal grows. Use this space for your ideas. Brainstorm words that describe baby animals and draw pictures.

Quick Tip

Use books, magazines, or websites to find pictures and names of baby animals. Choose animals that interest you for your list.

CHECK IN 1 2 3 4

Plan: Choose Your Topic

Writing Prompt Write a research report that explains how a baby animal grows. Go back to the ideas about baby animals that you brainstormed on page 91. Choose one of these animals to write about. Complete these sentences to help you get started.

My baby animal is _____

_____

I already know that _____

_____

I will look for other facts about this animal in _____

_____

 Purpose and Audience Authors write research reports to teach readers about the world. Think about why you chose the baby animal to write about. Then explain your purpose for writing in your writer's notebook.

Quick Tip

Your audience, or readers, may include your classmates. Think about how to interest your readers and what you want them to learn from your report.

Word Wise

Thinking about your audience will help you decide the words and tone to use in your writing. Use formal language when you are writing for a serious purpose, such as for essays, reports, and letters to your teacher.

CHECK IN 1 2 3 4

hirc83/E+/Getty Images

Plan: Research

COLLABORATE

Generate Questions Authors often plan their writing by asking questions about a topic. Look at the chart below. An author researched facts about a baby puffin bird. The author asked questions about the baby bird first and used the answers in a research report.

Quick Tip

Use words such as *who, what, where, when, why,* and *how* to write your questions.

Read the answers in the chart. Use these facts to complete the questions.

Question	Answer
What are the babies _____ ?	The babies are called pufflings.
_____ does the baby eat?	The parents feed them fish.
_____ does the baby change as it grows?	The baby's dark beak turns orange.

Plan In your writer's notebook, make a Question and Answer chart like the one above. Think about what sources you can use to find the answers. Use reliable sources, such as books, magazines, and websites.

CHECK IN 1 > 2 > 3 > 4

Draft

Order Ideas The author of "Eagles and Eaglets" describes events in an eaglet's life. Reread pages 15–16. These events can be put into a Sequence Chart. Complete this Sequence Chart.

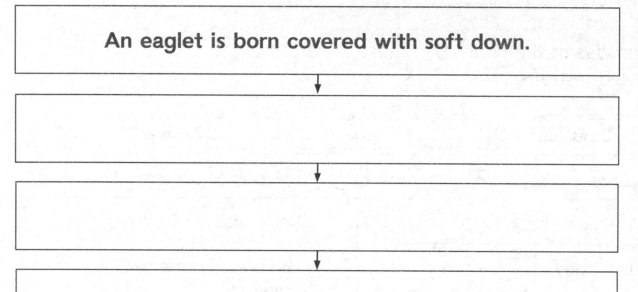

An eaglet is born covered with soft down.

In about five years, the eaglet becomes an adult.

Write a Draft Make a Sequence Chart in your writer's notebook. Use reliable sources such as books, magazines, and websites. Look over your list of questions. Then use this information to write your draft.

CHECK IN 1 2 3 4

predrag1/iStock/Getty Images

Revise

Sentence Fluency Writers use short and long sentences to add interest. Read the paragraph below. Use descriptive words and details to revise it. Make sure you use both short and long sentences to make the writing more interesting.

Quick Tip

You can use details you have read on page 13 of "Eagles and Eaglets" and your background knowledge to help you revise the paragraph.

Eagles build nests. Eagles lay eggs. The mother sits on her eggs.

The eggs hatch. The parents watch the nest.

_____

_____

_____

_____

_____

Revise It's time to revise your draft. Make sure you have some short sentences and some longer sentences to keep your writing interesting.

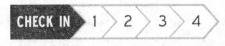

Revise: Peer Conferences

COLLABORATE

Review a Draft Listen carefully as a partner reads his or her work aloud. Begin by telling what you like about the draft. Make suggestions that you think will make the writing stronger.

Partner Feedback Write one of your partner's suggestions that you will use in the revision of your text.

Based on my partner's feedback, I will _____

_____

_____

After you finish giving each other feedback, reflect on the peer conference. What was helpful? What might you do differently next time?

_____

_____

Revision Use the Revising Checklist to help you figure out what text you may need to move, add to, or delete. Remember to use the rubric on page 99 to help you with your revision.

Remember to use the rubric on page 99 to help you with your revision.

Quick Tip

Use these sentence starters to discuss your partner's work.

The details in your draft helped me...

How about adding more facts about...

I have a question about...

✓ Revising Checklist

- ☐ Does my report give facts in the correct order?
- ☐ Does it include words that show the correct order?
- ☐ Does it answer my questions about how a baby animal grows?
- ☐ Did I use both short and long sentences?

Edit and Proofread

When you **edit** and **proofread**, you look for and correct mistakes in your writing. Rereading a revised draft several times will help you catch any errors. Use the checklist below to edit your sentences.

Editing Checklist

- ☐ Do all sentences begin with a capital letter and end with a punctuation mark?
- ☐ Are nouns used correctly?
- ☐ Are plural nouns spelled correctly?
- ☐ Are commas used correctly?
- ☐ Are all the words spelled correctly?

List two mistakes you found as you proofread your text.

1 _____

_____

2 _____

_____

Tech Tip

When you type your text, choose a font that is easy to read. Usually, type that looks like print in a book is easier to read.

Grammar Connections

As you proofread, make sure the nouns you used are spelled correctly. Remember how the spellings of irregular plural nouns change, such as *child/children, man/men,* or *foot/feet.*

Publish, Present, and Evaluate

Publishing Create a neat, clean final copy of your research report. As you write your draft, be sure to print neatly and legibly. You may add illustrations, a diagram, or other visuals to make your published work more interesting.

Presentation Practice your presentation when you are ready to present your work. Use the Presenting Checklist to help you.

Evaluate After you publish and present your research report, use the rubric on the next page to evaluate your writing.

Presenting Checklist

☐ Sit up or stand up straight.

☐ Look at the audience.

☐ Speak slowly and clearly.

☐ Speak loudly so that everyone can hear you.

☐ Answer questions using facts from your report.

1 What did you do successfully? _____

_____

_____

2 What needs more work? _____

_____

_____

4	3	2	1
• uses factual information	• uses mostly factual information	• uses some factual information	• does not have much factual information
• follows a clear sequence and uses signal words	• follows a sequence and uses some signal words	• does not have a clear sequence and is missing signal words	• has a confusing order
• has a variety of sentence lengths	• has some variety of sentence lengths	• has limited variety of sentence lengths	• has no variety of sentence lengths
• is free or almost free of errors	• has few errors	• has many errors that distract from the meaning of the report	• has many errors that make the report hard to understand

Turn to page 89. Fill in the bars to show what you learned.

My Goal I can write a rhyming poem.

Expert Model

Features of a Rhyming Poem

A rhyming poem:

- has words that end with the same sounds.

- tells a poet's thoughts or feelings.

Analyze an Expert Model Studying "The Little Turtle" will help you learn how to write rhyming poems. Reread page 160 in the **Literature Anthology**. Answer the questions below.

Literature Anthology: page 160

In the first four lines of the poem, what two words rhyme?

_____

_____

What is the funny joke that the poet makes at the end of the poem?

_____

Plan: Brainstorm

Generate Ideas You will write a rhyming poem about an animal. Use this space for your ideas. Draw animals that help you think of what your poem will be about. Then write words that tell about some of the animals.

CHECK IN 1 2 3 4

Plan: Choose Your Topic

COLLABORATE

Writing Prompt Write a poem about an animal. Try to tell a story about the animal in your poem. Your poem should have at least four lines and rhyming words. Complete these sentences to help you get started.

The animal in my poem is _____

_____

My animal wants to _____

_____

A problem might be _____

_____

Purpose and Audience Authors write rhyming poems because they want to entertain their readers or share feelings. Think about what feeling you want your audience to have when they read your poem. Explain the feelings you want your readers to have in your writer's notebook.

> **Quick Tip**
> Your audience, or readers, may include your classmates or family. Most people like to read rhyming poems. As you write, think about why your audience will enjoy reading your poem.

CHECK IN 1 > 2 > 3 > 4

Plan: Word Choice

Precise Language When you write, include details about your topic that will create a clear picture for your reader. Precise words are exact words that make your meaning clear. Complete the word bank below by writing precise words that describe a fish.

Quick Tip

Precise language exactly describes something. It helps readers create images in their heads of what you are describing. It also makes your writing easier to understand.

Word Bank		
splashing	scaly	smelly
slippery	glimmering	fast
golden	gliding	slimy

 Plan In your writer's notebook, use a word bank like the one above. Fill it in with precise words about the animal in your poem.

Draft

Specific Details The author of "Gray Goose" gives many specific details to describe the goose and the baby. She includes details such as *webbed feet slapping* and *wild waddle.* These details make it easy to picture the goose. Notice the details the author includes about the gosling.

Now use this poem as a model to include specific details about the animal in your poem. Include words that rhyme as you describe the animal in your poem.

_____

_____

_____

_____

_____

Write a Draft Look over the Word Bank chart you made from page 103. Use it to help you write your draft in your notebook. Remember to use specific details.

CHECK IN 1 2 3 4

Revise

Rhyme Authors find the best rhymes by trying different words. Sometimes they have to change an idea several times. Read lines from poems below. Then revise the lines to include pairs of rhyming words.

There was a purple butterfly

that fluttered in the _____.

My dog likes to have fun.

He always tries to _____.

 Revise It's time to revise your draft. Read the draft and work on making the words rhyme.

Digital Tools

To learn how to hear your rhyming poem read aloud, watch "Record Audio." Go to **my.mheducation.com.**

Quick Tip

Say two words aloud if you are not sure they rhyme. Words that rhyme might not look alike. *Kite* and *sight* end in the same sound, but the sound is spelled differently.

 Tech Tip

Some websites can help you find rhyming words. Type in a word and you will see some suggestions. You'll have to make the words fit in your poem.

CHECK IN 1 2 3 4

Revise: Peer Conferences

COLLABORATE

Review a Draft Listen carefully as a partner reads his or her work aloud. Begin by telling what you liked about the draft. Make suggestions that you think will make the writing stronger.

Partner Feedback Write one of your partner's suggestions that you will use in the revision of your poem.

Based on my partner's feedback, I will _____

_____

_____

After you finish giving each other feedback, reflect on the peer conference. What was helpful? What might you do differently next time?

_____

_____

Revision Use the Revising Checklist to help you figure out what text you may need to move, add to, or delete. Remember to use the rubric on page 109 to help you with your revision.

Remember to use the rubric on page 109 to help you with your revision.

Quick Tip

Use these sentence starters to discuss your partner's work.

I was interested in the animal because...

I enjoyed this part of your poem because...

I have a question about...

✔ Revising Checklist

☐ Does my poem fit my purpose and audience?

☐ Does it include rhyming words that relate to the animal?

☐ Did I use details?

☐ Did I use exact words to express my ideas?

Edit and Proofread

When you **edit** and **proofread**, you look for and correct mistakes in your writing. Rereading a revised draft several times will help you catch any errors. Use the checklist below to edit your poem.

Grammar Connections

Sometimes one sentence in a poem is written on two lines. Make sure you use correct punctuation to help a reader understand your poem.

✔ Editing Checklist

☐ Did I use correct punctuation?

☐ Are words spelled correctly?

☐ Are apostrophes used correctly?

☐ Are possessive nouns used correctly?

List two mistakes you found as you proofread your poem.

1 _____

_____

2 _____

_____

Publish, Present, and Evaluate

Publishing Create a clean, neat final copy of your rhyming poem. As you write your final draft, be sure to print neatly and legibly.

Presentation Practice reading your poem when you are ready to present your work. Use the Presenting Checklist to help you.

Evaluate After you publish and present your rhyming poem, use the rubric on the next page to evaluate it.

1 What did you do successfully? _____

_____

_____

2 What needs more work? _____

_____

_____

_____

Presenting Checklist

- ☐ Sit up or stand up straight.
- ☐ Look at the audience.
- ☐ Read your poem with expression and feeling.
- ☐ Speak loudly so that everyone can hear you.
- ☐ Answer questions using details from your poem.

4	3	2	1
• has many details about an animal • includes four or more rhyming words • includes precise language • is free or almost free of errors	• has some details about an animal • includes some rhyming words • includes some precise language • has few errors	• is about an animal but lacks details • makes an effort to include rhyming words • makes an effort to use precise language • has errors that distract from the meaning of the poem	• does not focus on the topic • lacks rhyming words • does not include precise language • has many errors that make the poem hard to understand

Turn to page 89. Fill in the bars to show what you learned.

TAKE NOTES

Take notes and annotate as you read the passages "A Prairie Guard Dog" and "A Visit to the Desert."

Look for the answer to this question: *How do animals survive in their habitats?*

_____

_____

_____

_____

PASSAGE 1

NARRATIVE NONFICTION

A Prairie Guard Dog

It is summer, and I am on a journey. My trip is to a prairie. Many animals live in a prairie habitat. A prairie has a lot of grasses but few trees. This place has what prairie dogs need to survive.

It is early in the morning. First, I see a prairie dog. I name him Pete. He peeks his head out of his burrow underground. He looks around. Then Pete calls loudly to his family, "Yip!" He lets them know it is safe to come out. Soon four prairie dogs come out.

Pete is the guard dog. He is always looking around for danger. This allows the other prairie dogs to safely munch on grasses and seeds that grow on the prairie. They can also groom each other or work on their burrow.

Jeff Foott/Discovery Channel Images/Getty Images

Prairie Dog Burrow

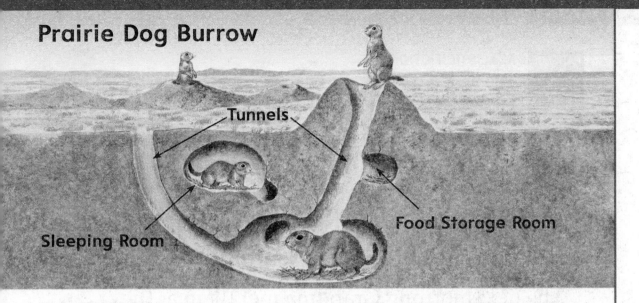

Tunnels

Sleeping Room

Food Storage Room

The Sun gets higher, and it is hot now. The prairie dogs slip into their deep burrow. This shelter protects prairie dogs from both predators and the heat. Tunnels, like hallways, lead to different areas. There is a sleeping room. There is a room used like a bathroom. The prairie dogs cover up roots and seeds in one room. Later, they eat the food buried there.

I keep watching the burrow. Finally, the Sun begins to set and a different prairie dog peeks its head out. I name him Gary. Pete must be off duty. "Yip," Gary calls. The other prairie dogs come back out to eat and play until the Moon is high in the sky. Then they go to sleep in their burrows.

TAKE NOTES

PASSAGE 2   REALISTIC FICTION

A VISIT TO THE DESERT

This summer vacation Tim and his family went to visit Grandma in Nevada.

"Grandma is eager to see you," Mom said. "She can't wait to take you on a desert hike."

The next morning Grandma met them at the airport. Then they drove to the desert. As they hiked, Grandma explained that the animals find ways to adapt to the hot desert weather. Tim wondered if he could get used to the desert climate.

"Wow," Tim said, "look at that! The turtle carries its home on its back!"

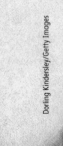

Grandma smiled at Tim's excitement. "Actually," she said, "that's a desert tortoise. It looks for the shade made by the shadows of rocks. That's how it cools off. He burrows underground to get away from the heat." The tortoise disappeared into its burrow.

Just then a large jack rabbit hopped by. Grandma explained that its large ears help it stay cool. She pointed out a cactus and other plants that it eats.

"These animals are so unlike the animals at home!" Tim said. He had forgotten about the desert heat.

"Some animals stay cool by sleeping during the day. Then they hunt at night," said Grandma. A Great Horned Owl hooted above them. Grandma said, "It will soon be time for the owl to hunt."

"Which means it's time for us to head back," Dad added.

"Aw, this hike went by too fast," Tim said. They asked Tim about the heat. "What heat?" Tim asked. "I've adapted!" Everyone laughed.

TAKE NOTES

Compare the Passages

Talk About It Reread your notes from "A Prairie Guard Dog" and "A Visit to the Desert." Talk with a partner about what you learned about how prairie dogs and desert animals survive in their habitats.

Cite Text Evidence Fill in the chart with details from the texts and pictures that describe each habitat. Then write details that tell how animals survive in their habitats.

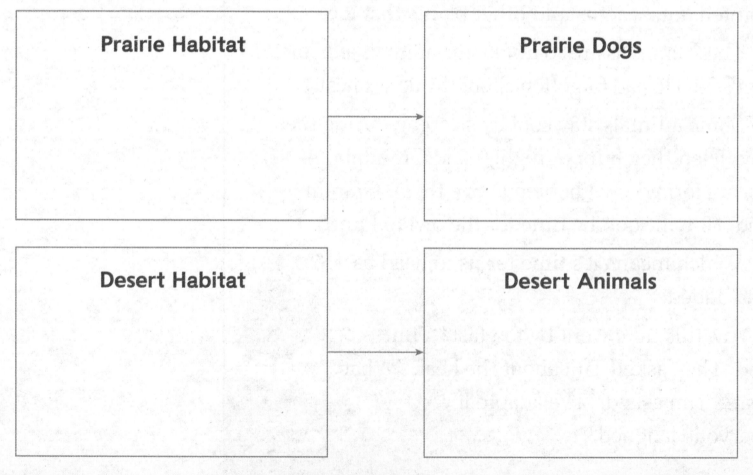

Prairie Habitat

Prairie Dogs

Desert Habitat

Desert Animals

How do animals survive in their habitats?

 Talk About It Look at the graphic organizer on page 114. Talk about how the basic needs of the animals are similar. Discuss how each animal is able to survive in its habitat.

Write Prairie dogs and desert animals are able to survive

in their habitats because _____

_____

_____

> **Quick Tip**
>
> Use these sentence starters to describe the habitats and basic needs of prairie dogs and the desert animals.
>
> *Both prairie dogs and desert animals need...*
>
> *They also need...*
>
> *Both habitats give the animals...*

 Combine Information

Why is it important for habitats to meet the needs of the animals that live there? What other kinds of animal habitats do you know about? How do they meet the needs of the animals that live there?

CHECK IN 〉 1 〉 2 〉 3 〉 4 〉

Habitat Poster

Work with a partner. Use print or online sources to create habitat posters that show habitats and the animals that live there.

- Explore habitats. Choose at least two habitats.

- Find out what animals live in each habitat.

- Research the types of plants that grow there.

- Learn how the animals meet their needs for food, water, and shelter in their habitat.

- Make a poster. Draw and label each habitat and the animals that live there.

Write two sentences comparing the habitats and the animals that live there.

Examples of habitats are forests, grasslands, wetlands, and oceans. When you create your poster, you may include where the habitat is located.

_____

_____

_____

_____

Go back to "A Visit to the Desert" on pages 112–113. Talk about how you would create a habitat poster for the story's desert setting.

Informative Paragraph

Work with your partner. Look back at the two habitat posters you created. Talk about the two different habitats. Choose one habitat you would like to write about. Write its name on the line below:

_____

Now write an informative paragraph that tells how the habitat meets the needs of animals. Include details that give the following information:

- how the animals find water and food

- where the animals find shelter

_____

_____

_____

_____

_____

Quick Tip

Use these sentence starters to organize the ideas in your paragraph.

- *Many animals live in...*

- *This animal finds food...*

- *It gets water...*

- *The animal finds shelter...*

My Goal I can read and understand science and social studies texts.

TAKE NOTES

Take notes and annotate as you read "Florida Panther National Wildlife Refuge" and "Monarch Butterflies on the Move."

Look for the answer to this question: *How does the map help you understand important details in each passage?*

PASSAGE **1** EXPOSITORY TEXT

FLORIDA PANTHER
NATIONAL WILDLIFE REFUGE

Not many Florida panthers live in the wild today. Florida's big cat is in trouble. But a government group is working to change this. The U.S. Fish and Wildlife Service takes care of wildlife and habitats. The group is helping the population, or number, of Florida panthers grow.

Once, Florida panthers lived in a large area. They had kittens in many parts of the South. This breeding range spread across eight states. Today, it is much smaller. The area is less than 5 percent of that size. The big cats can only be found in South Florida.

fotoguy22/iStock/Getty Images

To help save Florida panthers, the U.S. Fish and Wildlife Service created a refuge. It is protected land. It is at the center of their habitat. With their habitat protected, they can find food and places called dens to have kittens.

Without a habitat in Florida, these panthers would no longer live in the wild. Our big cat is an umbrella species. This means that we protect many other types of animals when we preserve the Florida panther's habitat.

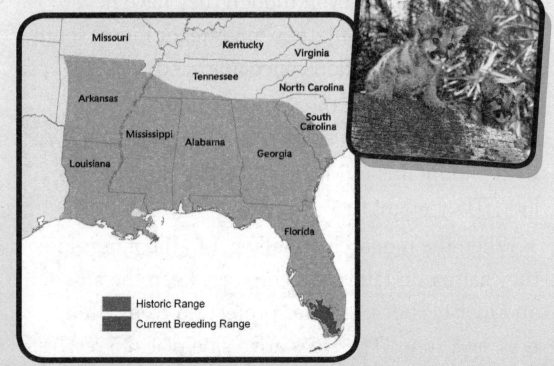

Missouri

Kentucky

Virginia

Tennessee

North Carolina

Arkansas

South Carolina

Mississippi Alabama

Georgia

Louisiana

Florida

■ Historic Range
■ Current Breeding Range

(l)U.S. Fish and Wildlife Service; (r)Rene Frederic/age Fotostock Wildlife Service

TAKE NOTES

_____

_____

_____

_____

_____

_____

_____

_____

_____

_____

_____

_____

_____

MONARCH BUTTERFLIES ON THE MOVE

Would you be able to find the place where your great-grandparents lived? Would you be able to find the place without looking at a map or knowing the name of the place?

Monarch butterflies do this. The butterflies travel to the same places, even though they have never been there! In the fall, they migrate, or move, south where older generations once migrated.

Monarchs west of the Rocky Mountains fly to California. Monarchs east of the Rocky Mountains fly to mountains in Mexico. The trip to Mexico is long. They might fly 2,500 to 3,000 miles!

When the monarchs finally get to the mountains, they gather on tall trees. The trees keep the air cool and moist. They also offer protection from wind, rain, and snow. The trees are a safe place to rest.

Butterflies, Lisa Thornberg/E Plus/Getty Images

In the spring, the days are warmer and longer. Monarch butterflies begin to leave the trees and fly north.

The monarchs search for blooming milkweed plants. They lay eggs on these plants. Caterpillars hatch from the eggs. They eat the milkweed plants. Soon, the caterpillars become orange and black butterflies. The children of the monarch butterflies continue the journey back north.

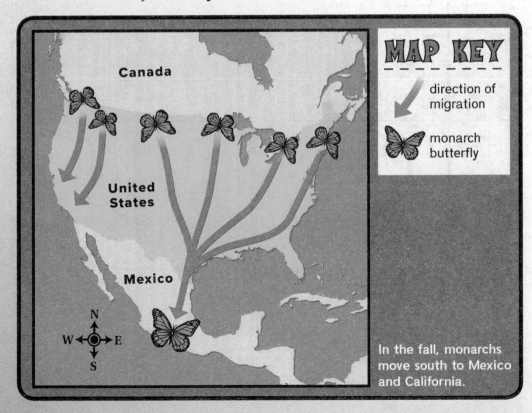

MAP KEY

→ direction of migration

🦋 monarch butterfly

In the fall, monarchs move south to Mexico and California.

Canada

United States

Mexico

N
W ← → E
S

Lisa Thornburg/E Plus/Getty Images

TAKE NOTES

Compare the Passages

Talk About It Reread your notes on the two passages. Talk about the important details in the text that each map shows. Discuss how the maps help you understand these details.

Cite Text Evidence Fill in the chart with what you learned from the maps and map elements.

	The map shows ...	The labels show ...	The map key tells ...
Passage 1			
Passage 2			

SOCIAL STUDIES

? How do the map and map elements help you better understand the text?

COLLABORATE

Talk About It Look at the graphic organizer on page 122. Talk with your partner about information in the text that the map shows. How do the maps help you understand these important details?

Write The maps and map elements help us better

understand the text by _____

_____

_____

_____

(page 122)

✂ Combine Information

How do map elements help us better understand maps? How do maps help us understand what the authors explain in a text? Talk about how the maps supported the authors' points or made them stronger.

> **Quick Tip**
>
> Use these sentence starters to talk about what the maps show.
>
> *The maps show...*
>
> *I can see on the map...*
>
> *This helps me understand...*

CHECK IN 1 2 3 4

Unit 2 · Connect to Content   123

Map of Your School Neighborhood

COLLABORATE

Work with a partner. Create a map of your school neighborhood. Follow the steps below:

1. First, draw and label streets you know.

2. Next, draw your school.

3. Then, draw familiar places near your school. These could include a park, a library, a supermarket, or a post office.

4. Last, draw a compass and a map key. The map key can show a small drawing of the school on the map with the label *school* next to it. It can show small drawings of other familiar places with labels too.

Now write sentences telling what your map shows and how the compass and map key help readers better understand the map.

_____

_____

_____

_____

Reflect on Your Learning

Talk About It Reflect on what you learned in this unit. Then talk with a partner about how you did.

I am really proud of how I can _____

_____

_____

_____

Something I need to work more on is _____

_____

_____

_____

Share a goal you have with a partner.

My Goal Set a goal for Unit 3. In your reader's notebook, write about what you can do to get there.